Rivers Within Us

Poems by

Sandy Coomer

Published by Unsolicited Press
www.unsolicitedpress.com
Copyright © 2017 Sandy Coomer
All Rights Reserved.
Unsolicited Press Books are distributed to the trade by Ingram.
ISBN: 978-1-947021-06-8
Cover Design: In-house UP team
Photo Credit: Richard Sparkman

This book is lovingly dedicated to my sisters,
Laura Spencer Higgins and Kelly Spencer Posey.

Rivers run strong in them both.

Table of Contents

Tributaries	1
Part One	3
River Man	5
Current	7
The River	9
Wabash	10
Collage	12
If Only	14
Revival	16
Eucharist	18
The Black Ant	20
Anthem	22
From Lightning	24
Driving West Across Montana	25
Synesthesia	27
Bones	29
Unnamed Road	31
Part Two	33
Red Summer	35
Fair Park	37

Dream Whisperer	39
The Ladder	40
Oracle	41
Friends	43
Kyrie Eleison	45
Signs of Wealth	46
Lost	48
Caldwell Lane	49
Most of All	50
Epiphany	52
Did I Ever Tell You	54
Dimension of a Dream	55
Rivers Within Us	57
Notes	59
Acknowledgements	61
About the Author	63
More from Unsolicited Press	64

Rivers Within Us

Tributaries

River of the secret longing,
      river of the silken whisper,
carry me to the garden shed
and break the lock,   break the window
and use the glass to cut
      a swath of usefulness in me.

River of the sallow flesh -
      I don't want to be beautiful.
I'm content to be wild.
Southward river, indigo deep,
      set a sail on me.

River of the shattered roses,
      river of dark dreams
that lead me to the bitter sea of salt and green,
      see me.

River of the past, rescue me.

River of the sultry heat and malcontents,
      divine me,   find my iron.
River of the crinkled lake, unbraid me.

River of the crying steeples,
      river of the wine-warped field,
river of moonlight and silver birds
and every blue-touched wing,

    drag me to the center,
let the current catch me
in its open mouth,   taste me, swallow me,
let me live on the tongue
like bittersweet citrus,   like arugula and chard.

River of the soul-white swan,
    the lilacs and cucumbers wait for harvest.
The blackberries bow the shrub
and bears rip through thorns.
The soul-starved earth sinks beneath you,
    the wind hurls silver spears,   whips
the white foam of your unwinding.

I want to be
    rivulet and spring,
porous limestone shelf,
floating log   flinging itself
far from the tree it used to be.

Part One

Rivers of living water will flow from within . . .

John 7:38

River Man

     We swam the Tennessee River
with your dead eyes open to us, silent within
willow fronds on the surface, green tendrils
reaching down.
     Your body hung there, suspended
for days. No one knew you, or counted you missing,
or turned the shore end over end to discover
your ending.

It was an accident – finding you.

     The rescue boats weren't sent
for you, nor the lights on the early dawn striping the water
meant to catch a shadow, a silhouette, dark and human-like
among the rushes.
     Swimmers, safe in our suits,
watched over by so many guardians, glided by
in our ignorance without a single
prayer for you.

This was your funeral procession.

     Bless the river minnows and the fat blue catfish,
the bull frogs on the stones sloshing a drunken song,
the sound of the current patiently tugging
your pant leg,
     the sun's rays that recognized
your face as earth, not water, not meant to float so still,
thick and water-boarded, tangled in a journey of silence

and night.

You were a sentence in the newspaper.

    Unloaded from your house
of sticks after the last swimmer passed – no name,
no hometown – your cells swollen, sloughing into the vast
throat of river,
    you were the voice
imagined in our watery dreams, trapped beneath glass,
the liquid breath over the words we finally found for you
on the shore.

Current

After the party, because someone said river,
we crammed eight people into a two-door Camry

and sped to find one, all of us a little drunk, except,
perhaps, the driver. Two girls curled around each other

in the passenger seat and I was pressed into a back corner,
part of a hip-locked quartet, with your body lying across us.

Though you and I were barely friends, the close space
between our faces erased formality. I could lean forward

and touch your mouth with mine, your eyes flashing
with the street lights as we drove overfilled, overburdened

with the life we chose. How far do we have to go to really
see someone, lines on the skin and lines between who we are

and who we want to be? We juggle our fear of truly seeing
with the fear of being truly seen.

You and me against the window - for a moment we knew
we were more than confessions and recited biographies

until the river with its rush and swell scared us
back into our bodies. It was black on the edge of the road

and below us the water tumbled from long-ago
mountain anthems. The air we breathed was icy and dark

and not at all the epiphany we hoped it would be.
The next day, when you and I passed on the street,

we looked the other way, as if to see each other
up close again would be too risky to our grounded selves.

We won't think about the river and its boundless current.
We try hard to forget who we almost were.

The River

The river rides high tonight, four days
of rain filling the hollows, spreading
the spongy sod until it is full – too full –
and what it cannot hold runs wild.

The murky brown-black of a living soul,
the gravid voice that is labored, shrill -
what do we know of a river's dream
to escape its tall walls and wander?

And what did we know of your dreams,
how it was to be young, to want
so much beyond what you could reach,
what did we know of the strength

of the current within your veins?
You and the river are one tonight,
both of you swollen and raw, a naked
gash against the earth and still wanting,

dark wanting on the bank
where the river spit you out. The land
seeps out of your eyes, all the sorrow
and suffering, the high dead words spilling,

the voiceless speech of dreams
spreading your heart
until it is full—too full.
And what it cannot hold runs wild.

Wabash

The river catches the afternoon sun,
      low and shielded by the cold leftovers
           from yesterday's rain.

Tracks in the sand spell coyotes and deer, a lone runner
      and me, boot-edged and heavy with solitude.
           A place is not complete

without its people, whetted by words, and bound
      by conversation, but perhaps this river speaks
           for us all, its voice

stirring with swell, its channels old and curling like ribbons
      as it traces the cutoffs and oxbows charmed
           by Indiana's terrain.

Frogs are blessed in river mud, herons exalted
      by the sinking sun, and I watch fish flap, ride
           the murky face

with bone white logs and microcosm as the river twists east,
      then west, then south, taking twice as many miles
           to arrive as it needs to.

I stand still as history spears past - the birth of small streams,
      a trickle from a hidden spring, mountain snow-melt
           seeping into caverns ready

to burble and surge a wider course. Journeys are like that.
      The first step spreads into something more until it
            roars against the paths

planned for it, sweeps the husks of resistance down as it
      thrusts its way through. If this river could hear,
            I wonder if it would lift a little

at my passing near, if it knows me by my breath along
      the rocky shore, alone with all the voices of my past.
           Or does a river content itself with its own

and nothing more, the way I sometimes do, when my wild
      heart journeys toward all the selves I am, and my feet
           have no choice but to follow.

Collage
For Bill

Remember how we used to sit in the sun
and invite light into our skin, cooled
by a west wind teasing the beech trees?
You would say something sharp –
about politics, about global warming
or corporate greed, about how God would hate
the religion we name to excuse our wars.
And I would think about your voice
as it rides the dips and ridges of your convictions,
and the way you pause, let the words rise
as high as they can before gravity loops them,
pulls them down with your solemn nod.
Once we walked through the woods
near the lake and you named
the turtles and ducks their proper names –
Red-Eared Slider, Lesser Scaup –
as if to speak of them less formally
would somehow take from them
their earned status, their justified honor.
I told you how I make birds
with torn paper, glue each strip down
on canvas, irregular and amorphous,
until the shape of the bird pushes out
from within the layers, I offered each one
a moniker for its wings – Beauty, Memory, Joy –
and you nodded as if it was a royal thing I did,
creating from the leftovers, the rubble,
like we all do every day when we wake.

Today I sit on the floor and the morning sun
presses warmth like a quilt across my legs.
I read your poems again, lifting them
off the page with your remembered voice.
Again, I'm struck with how beauty
is sometimes unbearable, how certain words
tear the breath from me, and others sew
the wounds, each piece of me reclaimed
in the silence.

If Only

I'm down to these words.

If only the river cut straight
across the land like roads, pitched
north to south, simple, expected.

If only the hammer could pound
the mountain down, the screwdriver
lock the pieces together.

If only wine tasted more like
cherries, the cheese like smoke,
we would not be standing here
in this broken doorway.

If only the pine tree hadn't died,
the one beside the pond.

If only we hadn't paid the tree service
four hundred dollars to cut it down,
grind the stump and branches.

A dead tree is an eyesore, you said.

A dead tree is a tragedy.

The space the tree left is now filled
with light. That's a good thing, you said.

Except for the shade-loving plants.
Except for the cool water fish that swim
in the pond. Except for the salamanders
that slink wetly below the rocks.

If only I had known the right words.
If only the dictionary app had worked.
If only I had cell service out here
in the wooded wild, I could have called you
and said, if only you would wait.

But you would have said you've waited
long enough.

If only my heart would beat slower.
If only someone had warned me how this
would feel.

If only I could hear beneath your silence,
read the words behind your eyes.

We leave each other to our privacies.

If only we weren't so good at that.

Revival

You were born sick
the preacher says and I can't help but notice
he doesn't include himself in that distinction.
I assume he was born well, the apple
among the snakes.

It wouldn't make me feel better
if he said we were *all* born sick. That sounds
rather final and depressing, like there's little hope
of anyone digging out. Maybe that's how it is.
We carry shovels

and dress in lies and illusions,
our truest selves shadowed under elephant clouds.
And what about those elephants, white or pink or gray,
and the ostriches in the same field –
wide body, little head,

but a neck that could break your arm.
Does it matter that entire species are nearly extinct,
while snakes multiply in the dark and mossy
underneath, their eggs like small pale stones
spilling wet coils.

The preacher's long neck and dewy face drips,
and there are sweat rings under his arms.
His voice is heavy with emotions as he slaps
our faces with final judgements—
sick, born sick, too sick—

until we are swollen like the sky.
A smothering heaven spills its guts
as the preacher's Adam's apple bobs damnation,
the words pounding like elephants
or ostriches.

Eucharist

I study the burnt side
of a potato chip that depicts
the face of Jesus in its dark edges.
I've heard of God spreading the love
in pancakes and quesadillas,
popping a grin among flour and oil,
but a mass-produced junk food snack
doesn't seem like the best venue for the Savior.
I'd rather see Jesus in the dimpled marble
of a labyrinth in Chartres,
eleven rings of meditation and mirth,
or hear him in the clear soprano
of a boys' choir, the voices not yet tuned
with the longing of manhood. I want
my Jesus to be pure, with no
hydrogenated oils, caramel color,
or yeast extract.

But this potato chip Jesus seems
genuine. I lay it on the counter
and wait for it to speak wisdom –
like the orange that, when split, confides
the crucifixion, like the pierogi that sold
on Ebay for a thousand bucks with a face
that spoke of sacrifice and suffering.
I want authentic doctrine. I want
the cross and the foundation and the rock.
I want everything –
the orange, the pierogi, the bass,

the tenor, the path through the labyrinth
and out again, the bread,
and the anointing oil, the burnt smile,
and the eyes – so hollow, so broken –
I might mistake them
for my own.

The Black Ant

We see it almost at the same time –
a tiny black carpenter ant
on our dead uncle's white suit.

Your eyes widen with a strange mix
of horror and amusement, as if you
can't decide whether to laugh or cry.

We stare at the ant as it makes its way
up the lapel and around the collar, both
of us willing the other to do something

before it disappears around our uncle's neck.
Perhaps because you're the oldest
and are used to such responsibility,

you lean into the slick black marble casket,
holding your breath, wrinkling your nose,
mumbling a rigid curse

at the funeral director's lack of attention,
pinch the ant between forefinger and thumb,
crumble it, crumb-like, to the floor.

We tell each other it came from one of the plants,
but we know the ant was doing what ants do –
dragging death away straight through

the living, even as death poses
huge and incalculable.
We try not to feel so small.

Anthem

I wake to the sound of birds
high-pitched and screeching
like they are crushing
unwelcome syllables in their throats.

I try not to be angry on days like this

when the language of the world
nimbly reminds me
that some words carry a weight
lead-thick, a lexicon of worry

like *biopsy* and *scan* and *mass*.

I am trying to be comfortable
with being uncomfortable, to blink
when darkness glooms like a chanted spell.

I try to believe in science, or at least in hope,
even though I can't wrap my arms around either.

I try to remind myself it's just
the medicine that tastes metallic in my mouth,
it's just the invisible beams of a strange kind of light
that razors through me.

These things aren't permanent. But then, neither am I.

I try to get comfortable with that.

I'm relying on language to get by. I pack my body
with sound, silky slips of words like *invisible*

and *honest* and some with an edge
like *ardent* and *practice* and *abide*.

The birds calm in the moist blush of dawn.
They won't latch me to their wings
and take me with them when they fly.

I try to get comfortable in the dirt.

From Lightning

let us
count seconds to the thunder.
That's how many miles away
the storm brews. This is scientific,
a truth distilled, drop by sticky drop.

Komodo Dragons
taste with their tongues, waving
their heads back and forth
in favorable wind, detecting death,
fresh flesh to feed upon.

In our frailty, we rinse thoughts
in new rain, tilt our head
to view the elemental, the pictures
in the science magazine,
the words

part curse, part love letter,
part hopeless, part affirming.
We watch the slow drip
and think poetry and paranoia,
words and windows

both trying to open.
We are dragons –
and the sentence serves
as a halo, the world a sort of storm
feeding upon itself.

Driving West Across Montana

Thinking of your father, you stop at the casino in Lame Deer
with the intention to play Blackjack.

From the parking lot, you watch a tall woman in cut-off
denim shorts carry a toddler and a liter bottle of water

as she walks the side of the highway.
The road is hot and straight but the casino

wears a rounded roof and shelters swallows in its eaves,
little mud nests plastered into edges, holding on

with dry grasses curved like fingers. At the D & D
Trading Post next door, you could buy peanuts and oranges

if you wanted to, but you don't. Instead, you buy
Gatorade and a pack of gum. Whisky bottles

and beer cans pile like empty memories beside the door.
A flyer announces movie night at Chief Dull Knife College.

Motorcycles pass semi's on low hills despite the solid
yellow line, throw the love of Jesus at minivans and sedans.

Heat rises from the asphalt in blue waves. You are
a lone Black-eyed Susan, haunting the casino parking lot.

You don't go in.

You listen to the passing cars, the sound
of other lives hurtling through - a whoosh, a wheeze.

Rosebud Creek dries like a cough caught
in the high-up lungs of the river it tries to feed.

You snap a photo of clouds with your cell phone,
the pale blue sky between them blank in the frame.

What you remember when you kneel behind the casino,
share your father's ashes with sagebrush and prairie grass

is the circling swallows, churring a dry-throated screech,
and the sky, desperately unfolding itself

into schisms of beauty.

Synesthesia

I woke up with the word *Chrysalis* in my mouth
and it tasted like cinnamon, distilled and concentrated
in oil. In high school, we carried vials and toothpicks
in our pockets, burned our tongues between classes,
our lips blistered and peeling. It made speech difficult,
reasoning even harder. We mumbled with swollen words.

I wrote my name in the air and it sounded like *Gravedigger*.
I wasn't sure I heard right, and it would not
repeat itself even when I begged. Some names
carry within them an elemental truth:
Obsidian and *Silence*, *Alstroemeria* and *Forget-Me-Not*.
Even *Cinnamon* has a way with fire.

If you hold a feather under your tongue, you can know
what it's like to float on air, unstrung and boundless.
The oil of flight tastes a little like *Windfall*, and *Deep Diving*,
but also *Broken Arrow*, and *Iron Breath* and *Bitter Weed*.
I spit it out, rub it into paste between my fingers.
My own whisper flutters in my hands.

If you know what color C major is, you will always
find a symphony in your closet. When I wear red,
my father hums Mozart. Play E flat minor and Prokofiev's
landscape of somber greens foreshadow a future
war. A web of deception, sticky and silky, arcs
through skies gray as stones and just as hard.

I want to hold the word *Ambivalence* in my palm
and carry it to the small corner where you sit alone.
I offer you this – a woven nest lined with fur, discovered
in a hollow of vines, the dusky scent of dry mushrooms,
a smooth raw pearl. A butterfly, wet with effort
and churning with foam, wears eyes on its wings.

Let me tell you what I see with them.

Bones

I have an affinity for old graveyards cradling centuries
of dead, long white bones silent beneath the dark earth.

I gaze at obelisks, Gothic tablet stones, and bevel markers
engraved with names and dates, some barely readable:
faithful husband, beloved wife, thy loss is deeply felt.

My daughter and I walk the path through the cemetery
of our town. She hints at ghosts –images of undead rising.

I feel the peace of unfolded years, slow breezes and rest
beneath trees, but I am much closer to such things than she is.
She doesn't understand how a name issues a place,

and a place, a marker of belonging. She doesn't yet grasp
how the sun glinting through branches can be holy,

how even plastic roses can have an austere beauty.
Some things are not spoken much – that one day I want to lie
in the circle of my ancestors, covered with Tennessee soil.

I imagine my daughter remembering how the bones
in our faces shaped our cheeks in similar ways,

our chins rounded, the sockets of our eyes a breath too wide
for beauty, our shoulders a bit too narrow for strength,
our hips fit for babies, our ankles able to carry it all.

But maybe not. Maybe she will walk these paths alone
and mark the epitaphs of remembered lives as sacred words.

Or maybe she will hold the hand of her own child
and whisper to him the lives that came before, murmuring
with the same words the trees use to coax the sky:

wander the slant hill with me, feel the bones
underneath your feet.

Unnamed Road

A secret, this road
curving off a Tennessee highway.

Graveled, seldom traveled,
it carves a track through beech trees.

Satellites mark a gray line on the GPS,
but cannot pin a moniker.

The database spins
while I stop my car and listen

for all the names unknown and holy.
I tilt my head and view

the morning's sunrise map – poppy orange,
lipstick pink, berry red –

each color shouting its unique flame.
The GPS worries a warning – undesignated area.

I thrill at the danger, surge
on the open way before me,

sure it leads to where I need to go.

Part Two

*May what I do flow from me like a river,
no forcing and no holding back...*

Rainer Maria Rilke

Red Summer

All summer, you burned a ring
around our back yard, you not working like other dads,
and Mom at the department store selling shirts
and ties to the wives of men who did.
Her eyes were red and tired when she slipped
a ten-dollar bill into our dirty hands.

We'd been exploring the old red barn
behind the neighbor's house - red,
like your shoulders when you came in
from mowing the yard, the watery blisters
bubbling like fish breath in a silent pond,
red, like your face

when the words you wouldn't hold back anymore
flooded the kitchen floor and our mother
grabbed her purse and keys, slammed the door
behind her. She stood beside her car, her hand
on the roof as she counted her anger
from red, to orange, to yellow, to white.

Our eyes, on her back and arms,
willed her from the kitchen window
to find us worthy of her struggle.
We didn't know how to beg,
but when she reappeared,
we gave her back the crisp new bill

as if that small act of returning could influence
a future choice, as if the small wave of her hand
that meant *go play*, which sent us back to climbing
the loft to judge the world from a higher gaze,
could loosen the knots in our throats,
the tinny echoes of the words you threw.

When we, too, found a reason to come home again,
and found you with the red eyes of our mother
in the half-dark, pulling weeds from the tangle of iris,
we dropped to our knees beside you,
and watched the fireflies burn red promises
across the blank bed of night.

Fair Park

In my mind it is always summer in Nashville -
    even as my sister and I slip the fence
and stroll across asphalt,
    the bleak winter sky a backdrop
for Tilt-a-Whirl yellow, Cotton Candy pink.
    We stand at the ticket booth
like we used to years ago, when our small
    hands clutched a sack of R C Cola caps
and labels from cans of Vietti Chili
    we'd trade for a strip of red tickets.
Dragging them on the ground, we'd eye
    the line at the Paris After Dark haunted house,
the padded thud of the bumper cars
    competing with pinball music from the arcade.
Now dormant, shadowed, we dream of a season
    that won't come again. No summer sun
to paint purpose on open gates. No organ-grinder's monkey
    fingering coins. No rides on the quaking Skyliner,
the wooden coaster than felt as secure as a house of cards.
    My sister says the merry-go-round horses
with the painted-on saddles and real leather reins
    sold at an auction, along with train cars
from the miniature railroad and the windmill
    from the Putt-Putt golf course.
What's left are the outbuildings, the low slung roof
    of the shooting gallery, the aluminum turnstile
set in concrete where the ponies were hitched
    and walked with their burden of child.
In our mother's house, our elementary report cards rest

  in a drawer, strung with E's and the Fair Park stamp
that proved we cashed in our brains
  for a little joy when joy was hard to come by.
A fickle winter sun impales the afternoon
  with faded Ferris Wheel orange, Ring Toss blue.
We edge back to life,
  the fence a boundary we won't cross again,
nor the memory, that dangerous ride.

Dream Whisperer

I tell the dream interpreter about tornados and my father.
    He says meaning is in the mind of the dreamer.
I say images flicker like filmstrips.
    He says they tumble through sleep's narrow tunnel
    and land at the base of the soul.
The talking horse from the TV commercial winks,
talks about violence. I remember the teeth,
biting the words like the bikini model
chomps a jalapeno double bacon burger,
sauce dripping down her chin. I think about symbolism.
    You must think less, see more, he says.
The tornados keep coming, dressed in burgeoning clouds,
wide as the swirling chasm to Hades, loud as a wolf's howl.
There is glass on the floor that cuts my feet. I walk in letters.
    You must walk over the words you want to say.
My father stands in front of the window, the wind pressing
a violent hand. The broken glass forms eyes, many eyes –
my father's and the storm's as the house shuts itself tight
against seeing.
    Did anyone die? the dream-man asks.
I answer, not yet.

The Ladder

*All this time I've been finding myself,
and I didn't know I was lost.*
        Avicii

I am the woman
shouting from the top rung
of the ladder,
  Follow me to the moon.
I take that next upward step
on faith, believing what Rumi said
about the way appearing
   as your foot falls upon it.

A bluebird has visited me every day
for fifty-six days. If that's not a sign,
I don't know what is.
   Blackberries ripen
each morning. I collect them in my hands,
finding myself inside the black globule mysteries
of sweet and sour, each berry tasting
   of universe and cosmos.

The bluebird's contagious joy
is a link to the wingless in me,
his song snagging
   that still-alive blink.
What grows between the spaces
is the difference between blackberries
and bluebirds. I don't need to be reminded
   I am still a seed.

Oracle

An octopus lingers over two square containers,
each marked with the flag of a country vying
for the World Cup championship.

Tentacles oscillate in psychic confusion
until the signal is clear, the choice made.
The octopus descends over one container,

snags a mussel, devours it. The prediction,
broadcast across the globe, portends victory
for the chosen, disaster for the rejected.

Hordes of hate letters pour into the aquarium –
death threats, calamari recipes, warnings of revenge.
Love letters, too, overfill the mail slot,

as well as oracle service requests for election outcomes,
the likelihood of marriage proposals, winning the lottery.
The octopus, eight legs undulating

in sea-water domain, floats undaunted by fame,
while we stretch for something to believe in,
something to fill

the hollow in our lives with a strategy more solid
than chance. We open our fists to the palm reader
who scans the seams in our hands for hidden significance.

We subscribe to the horoscopes, revel
when the solar eclipse erects Libra's love life,
when the alignment of Mars and Saturn

leads Sagittarius to new employment.
We watch for signs and omens, premonitions
and prophecy, and just when we despair

that nothing is worthy of faith, another miracle
juts through the clouds, and the odds tell us
this one is real—

like the octopus, one hundred percent correct
in his predictions, but if you can't believe the mollusk,
there's a parakeet in Singapore

eager to reveal your fate.

Friends

The mass of men lead lives of quiet desperation.
                              Thoreau

You're making friends in the psych ward. Even Bob,
who debates the therapists and uses the word *technically*
in most of his arguments, holds a certain charm
within his damaged soul. There's little else to do but mingle.
Otherwise, you tell me, this party would be a bust.

Bernard's family brings pizza on his last inpatient day.
Its perfume wanders the halls, draws napping Ken
from his room. Amen, Ken says, over and over, and though
no one appreciates his sermons, no one tells him to stop
preaching. In any public or private venue, there is
an undeniable form of etiquette.

Tyler wears girl's white Keds sneakers with the strings
removed and drooping navy sweatpants, also with the string
removed. You say he's a good guy, just a little lost.
Eileen fidgets nonstop, sidles up to you and asks you to pray
for her, adding that no one can imagine her pain.

I prepare for your witty comeback,
something with an expletive, but you look at her
like you know her, and when she asks
if she is bothering you, you answer *no*.
I bite the inside of my cheek until I taste blood.
Someone sobs in the therapy room.

Bob technically doesn't believe in therapy.
When asked how he's feeling, he says,
like a banana popsicle.
Sara, a twenty-year-old alcoholic, sits beside you
and rests her head on your shoulder. Planning a suicide
was exhausting. She still can't get enough sleep.

Three weeks ago, you held a knife against your veins
exacting pain. Now you hold a sort of stable calm.
You tell me it's no great feat to be strong
in this ward of mental misfits, but I see in your eyes
a sort of realization growing – where you've been,
where you want to go.

Kyrie Eleison

Baritone soloist, you sang classical music,
Schubert's Mass in G, Mozart's Requiem,
Latin words I couldn't understand
except *Christe*, or *Domine Deus*, or *Sanctus*
which you explained from the piano bench
those late nights I watched you practice.

Even today I can't reconcile
those words in your mouth,
the holy sanctuary filled with your voice,
when so often I heard you from a different angle,
short blunt syllables heaved
from your tight and angry throat.

I can't explain how I felt
sitting on the red velvet pew cushions,
the vaulted cathedral space
a place of praise and your face praising.
Perhaps it was the unaccustomed beauty,
how you stood so straight and sure

in your black tuxedo, your arms lifting
as the music rose and floated,
Kyrie eleison, miserere nobis,
as if there was a way out through
that vast ceiling fleshed with candlelight,
as if mere words could bring mercy.

Signs of Wealth

You floor the gas pedal and the Jaguar shifts
sleek pinions, roars as other drivers gawk.

I remember when we stared at our first house,
the aluminum siding not yet pinged and uneven.

We thought having two bathrooms would be
holy, and a yard, leveled by a bulldozer,

a haven where we would plant our forest.
Remember when I filled the flower bed

with geraniums and you scolded me
for spending money on flowers?

Remember when the shrubs along the porch
turned brown, infested by bag worms,

how we snipped each bag with scissors
and burned the pile? But that was before

we mowed goldenrod and Queen Anne's lace,
before the boxy Toyota died in the driveway

and you said someday you'd have a real car.
You polish the Jaguar with a special cloth

purchased online. Heads turn at the flash of power
and I squint as sunlight shifts on silver rims.

The light strikes with a somber haze.
I look at my hands but no prayer comes.

We contemplate changing churches,
straining for a god that fits this new faith.

Lost

How was it that in that moment
cries of pain from the dog,
hips crushed under our tire,
did not erupt like fire
from the chambers of our minds?

The argument, which moments before
seemed paramount, shriveled
to the size of a grimace.
Stopping to ask directions
from the farmer in his vegetable plot,

his dog licked the sweat
from our legs like we were a gift
when we were hollow and bare,
a bubble of clever words
and arrogance.

The farmer pointed us home, a direction
we couldn't see with our self-laden eyes
and the enamored dog, so open
to loving us, paid for our sin
with his broken spine.

The farmer said
you don't want to see this
as the shotgun spoke smoke
and something burned in our throats,
thick as bile.

Caldwell Lane

One day we will stand
      at the end of the driveway
and know there is nothing left of us
      in this house, the rooms filled
with other mementos, other treasures,
      our existence stripped clean.
And one day this street will only be
      a passage to get to the shopping mall
in Green Hills and we will top
      the small rise and look west
and try to remember how it felt
      to know something fully –
which side of the maple tree
      leads to the crooked limb fit for a throne,
how the patio puddles after rain,
      how, on windy nights, the keyhole
in the side door howls enough
      to spook us into believing in ghosts.
If anything is certain, let us speak it,
      fasten it to our seams with safety pins,
protecting it as the years tumble.
      It will be up to us to hold this –
the shift of light in the barnyard
      at a certain afternoon hour, the purple
violets by the stone wall, the back porch
      that smells faintly of apples
when you close your eyes and breathe.

Most of All

You come home and tell me
in your testing-the-waters voice
that it doesn't matter

but I want to tell you that it does.

The little words that seem so unimportant
and transient, that will be gone tomorrow
and never thought of again,

might be the most important words you ever say.

I won't go on about history and how
all the essential things are discovered
when we look back at them. I won't tell you now

that the secret gates are the ones

you've passed though over and over
and didn't recognize at the time how the ivy
hung waist level and roses crept up

the trellis of the dream you've been chasing.

The moment you say it doesn't matter
is the moment you are less than what you deserve
to be. What I am telling you is, yes

it matters, yes. All the hours and the pale

morning faces and the *mights* and the *supposes* –
they all matter. And the *I am's* and what you put
after that and everything you fear to put after that –

it matters, and the day

you put it all down, lay it out in the grass
and watch it weave together in the last light
of dusk, matters most of all.

Epiphany

Let this be a poem
in which no one thinks about death –
no starving children,
explosives in back-packs,
crimes plotted at dawn.
Let's think instead
about the moon streaming gold
against a singular snow,
little chirps the sparrows give
on their way to gather thistle seeds,
the acrobatic delight of falling leaves.
And let this be a poem
in which no one thinks about love –
no one drowns
in the pools of jeweled eyes
or drinks promises from a lover's mouth.
Let's think about different passions –
running across meadows full of poppies,
the cold smooth surfaces of river stones.
Let's think about the red roof of a barn,
how the sun burnishes the tin.
Let's think about the first breath
we took this morning on our way
to brush our teeth, how jeans
feel on our thighs, how we love rituals.
But no, not love. We weren't going to talk about that.
Let's just sit here and think about nothing
and let the clutter of our mind dissipate
in the stillness, and for one slow moment

be aware of our skin –
how it contains us,
how the brush of a feather's thinnest fringe
can make us shiver.

Did I Ever Tell You

I walked this way after
all the commotion was over
and people chose sides fiercely

and wore their hate like hats
over their faces so no one could see
their eyes? But I saw yours

and followed you, watching
you watch a line of ants, those
deliberate soldiers marching,

and I stopped when you stopped
to touch the fringe of an uncurled fern,
to lift a stone just to see what was

alive underneath.

Dimension of a Dream

The loon calls between the folds
of my breath. It lifts me, cradles,
like a mother with her child.
Tranquility brushes the astral plane
and I long for that tenderness again –
simple, enduring.

I float on the loon's back, across the lake
of my best intentions. How glossy black
the feather bed of dreams. How slim
the margin between light and dark.
If I open my eyes, might this be the time
I see the defining color of peace?

Words slip from the loon's throat
with haunting clarity – *where are you, where?*
I think I should know how to respond,
but I've never owned this place my heart
seeks. The soul outside its sleeve of flesh
is the borealis of a new dimension.

In the slant of the loon's red eye,
I am reflected back – a mirror
in a mirror. Always, the light gives
its own perceptions and I breathe again
in the eerie song – black and white,
day and night, high and low, life

and the death that becomes another
life in another time and place.
Will you miss me when I leave this slip
of love, my darling? Will you search
in the verdant gardens? Never mind.
I know where I am now —

here . . . here.

Rivers Within Us

We chase the steely wind that rises off the ridge,
dive for yellow leaves just beyond our grasp.
This is the game of luck we play, when any nod from God
might keep us safe one more day. Sometimes when we listen
to the world shudder around us, totter on its spindle-thin legs,
we grope like a child straining in the darkness for some sense
of light. We're desperate to see something kind
when we look into humanity's eyes, and fear we won't.

You find what you look for, someone said, and I think
that's mostly true. Still, I hope I'm surprised by turquoise
skies roaming the back of the storm, the sacred heart
of trillium daring to rise from the deeply-patched underneath.
Even something as simple as a blade of grass
braving the crack in a driveway is reason enough
to believe in miracles.

There are rivers within us –
galloping herds of horses, hummingbirds that beat
their tiny hearts millions of times between the bee balm
and sage. Any moment now, we may open a door and enter
a green field and the knot of dread will be untied.
The roots of a tree may curve beneath us and unearth
our heart. This is how much the world needs us.
The river may swing its wide current and catch us
in its arms, a small blue spear of joy welcoming us home,
while all around us the whole world whispers,
what took you so long.

Notes

"River Man" – 2014 Ironman Chattanooga - Around 8:30 a.m., just as the swimming leg of the competition was underway, a body was reported in the Tennessee River under the Olgiati Bridge. According to the Chattanooga Police, the person, unidentified at the time, had not been a competitor in the race (Nooga.com). The body was eventually identified and returned to family for burial (Times Free Press, October 2, 2014)

"Collage" – For poet and teacher, Bill Brown. My mentor and friend.

"Eucharist" – "22 People Who Found Jesus in their Food," (Buzzfeed, March 29, 2013)

"Synesthesia" - Synesthesia is a neuropsychological trait in which the stimulation of one sense causes the automatic experience of another sense. Synesthesia is a genetically linked trait estimated to affect from 2 to 5 percent of the general population. Contemporary models agree that synesthesia involves communication between regions of the cerebral cortex in the brain that are not otherwise connected in nonsynesthetes. (Encyclopedia Britannica)

"Fair Park" - Fair Park Amusement Park in Nashville, Tennessee opened in 1952 and survived through 1987 when competition from Opryland USA killed it. It featured the Skyliner roller coaster, the Paris After Dark haunted house, the Mad Mouse, Tilt-a-Whirl, bumper cars, hand cars, the Cyclone, pink & blue cotton candy, and an actual organ grinder with a little monkey that took money. Vietti Chili labels or RC Cola caps could get you a whole afternoon of rides. Fair Park also had a miniature golf course which held a tournament every Labor Day with the winner going to a national event. (Chip Curley at pbase.com)

"Oracle" - Paul the Octopus became famous for predicting the outcome of soccer games. He was the unlikely star of the 2010 World Cup when he correctly predicted the winners of eight matches. A resident of the Sea Life Centre in Oberhausen, Germany, Paul passed away peacefully in his tank on October 25, 2010. He was two and a half years old. (BBC News, October 26, 2010)

Acknowledgements

Grateful thanks and appreciation to the editors of the following publications within which these poems first appeared, sometimes in slightly different forms.

4Ink7 – "The Black Ant"
Apeiron Review – "River Man"
Big Muddy – "Dimension of a Dream"
Clementine Poetry Journal – "Revival"
Chautauqua Journal – "Anthem"
Courtyard of Winds – "Eucharist," "Dream Whisperer," and "Most of All"
Daphne Magazine – "Tributaries"
Icarus Down Review – "Did I Ever Tell You"
Heartbeat Literary Journal– "If Only"
Main Street Rag – "Red Summer"
Number One – "Wabash" and "Fair Park"
Pilcrow & Dagger – "Collage"
POEM – "Kyrie Eleison" and "Lost"
Poems on Loss Anthology, Little Lantern Press – "Caldwell Lane"
Qu Literary Magazine – "Driving West Across Montana"
Red River Review – "Friends"
Slant – "Oracle"
Spirit Wind Poetry Gallery – "From Lightning" and "The Ladder"
Treehouse – "Synesthesia"

"The River" was originally published in the collection, The *Presence of Absence*, winner of the 2014 Janice Keck Literary Award for Poetry.

I am indebted to the director and creative counsel of Rivendell Writer's Colony, Sewanee, TN, for the blessing of a Writer in Residence Fellowship in February 2016. Many of the poems in this collection were written and/or revised during my stay, including the title poem, "Rivers Within Us," which had been waiting for the magic and spirit of Rivendell to free itself from a tangled mind. I am most grateful.

About the Author

Sandy Coomer is a poet, artist, and endurance athlete. Her poetry has been published in numerous journals and magazines including *Hypertrophic Literary, Qu Literary Magazine, Now and Then – The Appalachian Magazine, Big Muddy,* and *Chautauqua.* She is the author of two poetry chapbooks: *Continuum* (Finishing Line Press) and *The Presence of Absence* (Winner of the 2014 Janick Keck Literary Award for Poetry). Sandy is a poetry mentor in the AWP Writer to Writer Mentorship Program and the founding editor of the online poetry journal *Rockvale Review.* She lives in Brentwood, TN.

More from Unsolicited Press

Unsolicited Press supports dozens of independent authors by publishing and promoting their work. If you enjoyed reading Coomer's poetry, then you may like:

Twice Told Over by Adela Najarro

Dick Cheney Shot Me in the Face by Timothy O'Leary

The Home Stretch by Michael Campagnoli

Animal Histories by Jerrod E. Bohn

Watching Ourselves by Mark Belair

www.ingramcontent.com/pod-product-compliance
Lightning Source LLC
Chambersburg PA
CBHW021451080526
44588CB00009B/788